THE LETTERS

FROM A TO Z

Rafael Loreto

 SEMILLERO

THE LETTERS. FROM A TO Z.

RUBIANO
EDICIONES

Depósito legal: CA2024000044
ISBN: 978-980-18-4297-2

Coordinación editorial
Elisabel Rubiano
Correción
Elisabel Rubiano y Richard Barrios
Ilustraciones
Andrea Martínez Pérez
Diseño gráfico
Carmen Maura Peralta

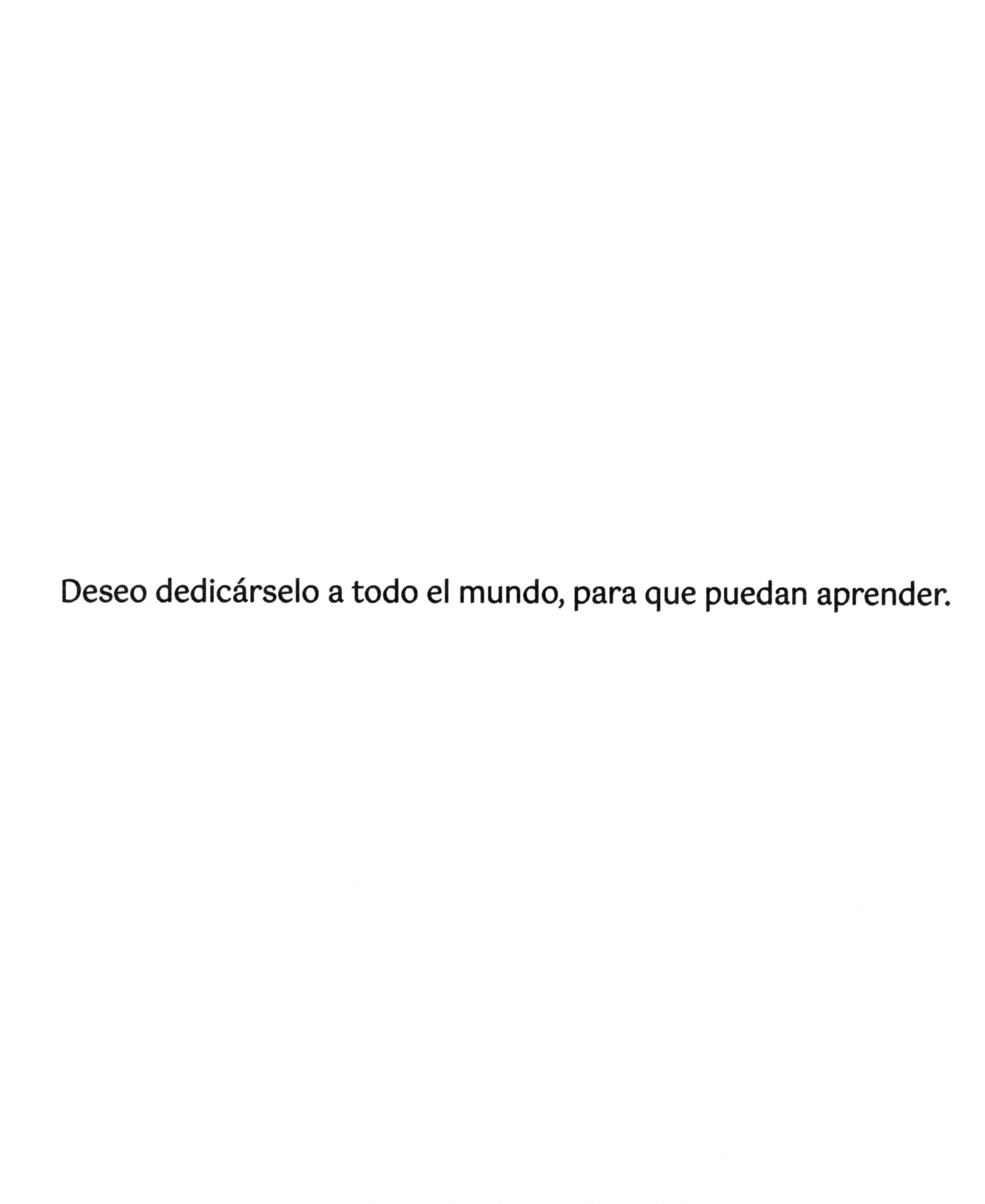

Deseo dedicárselo a todo el mundo, para que puedan aprender.

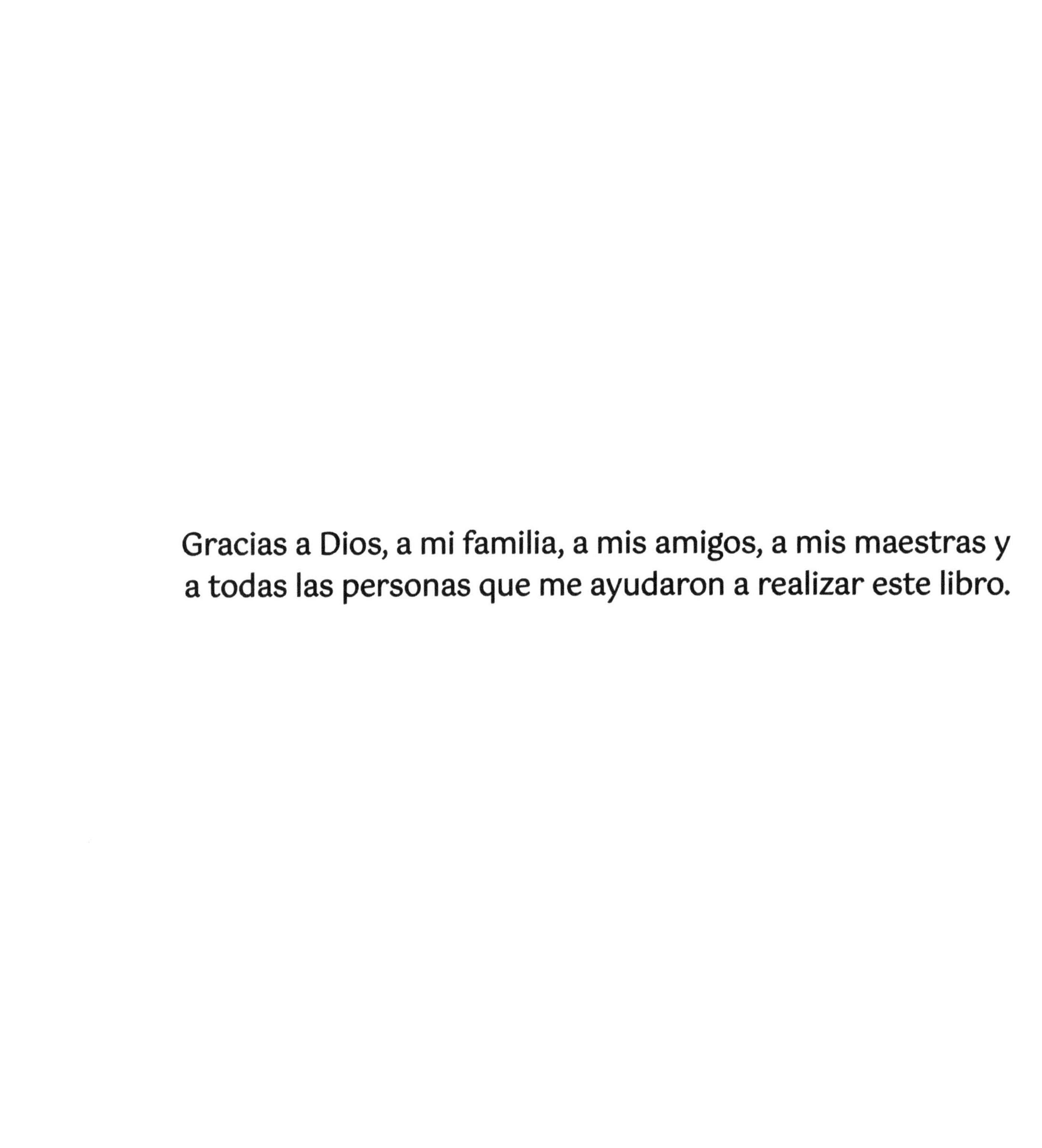

Gracias a Dios, a mi familia, a mis amigos, a mis maestras y a todas las personas que me ayudaron a realizar este libro.

THE LETTERS

These are all the letters from A to Z.

Do you wan't to learn them?
Thanks! **Lets go!**

This is amazing A,
It's in words like ant, apple,
arm, and also axe!
Let's move to bouncy B!

It's quite a sight...
But without B, you couldn't spell
boogie, bus, **banana** or even ball!

Crunch-up C!
now an exclamation Word that
starts with C like crunch
but there are also words like
cat, cape, cap and cup
can't exist without C!

Let's dance with dramatic D!

What a **dinosaur** book!
We use D in dog, dime, dirt, and
door, D marks the spot!

Exclamatory E!

There are not a lot of Words that start with E...

But there are some! Like **elephant**, egg, exit and edge!

I touched a poisonus **flower**! Fox, family, fun and friend! They all start with F!

Gamestastic and groovy G!
we use it in grass,
gorilla, gas & glassy g! what a
good and great G!

Say hi to H!

Also, some H words are silent... like honest! and H words are in hard, hippopotamus, **horse**, and have!

Incredible I!

We all love I... because it's a vowel and vowels are common!

I words are in igloo, **ice cream**, itchy bodies & ice...

Jump for J!

We all like jelly! And juice... and jaggery, jazz, joke & **jam**! Also jar...

Kick-up K!

This is K, which means... We like **kiwi**, kicking, kid & kite!! Which all of that we can do with K.

I love L!

Sing a lullaby... or even laugh... and you must like lakes, lightbulbs, **lemons**, and being lucky!

Marvelous M is coming on my side!
He likes mathematics, monkeys, mountain & making maps!

DON'T MAKE NOISE FOR N!!!
that's because N doesn't like loud noises...but other things like nuts, necks, nerves & name tags!

Okay O!
O is on middle of words like proxy and book... but its in octagon, oatmeal, one & oil!

Pupils in our eyes has two Ps! But other things like pat, pan, **pig** & pot starts with P!

Q is questrific!!
But sometimes it's in the middle,
like liquid and Q words starts in
quail, question, quick & quack!

Rock N'R! Because R ends in mirror... And chair! And starts in radishes, red, reindeer and **rats**!

S is the snappiest
sleeping time!!

Terrific T!

we all like T! because T can spell at the end fact! And at the start taxi, three, two & thinking!

Ultra-good U

U can spell much as uncle, ukulele, up & United States! A super popular country...

Now instead of
7 letters...
Where doing 5 letters!
Because there aren't
28 letters in the
alphabet let's go!

It's not bad V or not nice V... but very V! V starts in vacuum, viking, **vase** & voice! Vulicious!

Wonderful W!

Welcome to the W! it can spell a lot! :D, like where, we've, wack & **wax!**

We agree! Most X words end
sometimes, like t-rex! Starts in
xylophone, and **x-ray!**

Y ends for crazy and proxy... and it starts in yak, **yam**, yell & yeti!

I'll bet you'll like Z!
Because Z can spell much as zipper, zoo, zebra & zucchini!

Tengo 7 años, estudio 2do grado. Me encantan los planetas, los países, las banderas, el inglés. Soy el hermano mayor de Camila.

Me divierto mucho en los parques, jugando tenis, haciendo videos, animaciones y me gusta viajar.

Me levanto para ir al colegio, al regresar almuerzo y me preparo para asistir a mis actividades por las tardes, jugar y hacer mis tareas, me baño y ceno para dormir.

Los fines de semana salgo con mi familia o descansamos en casa.

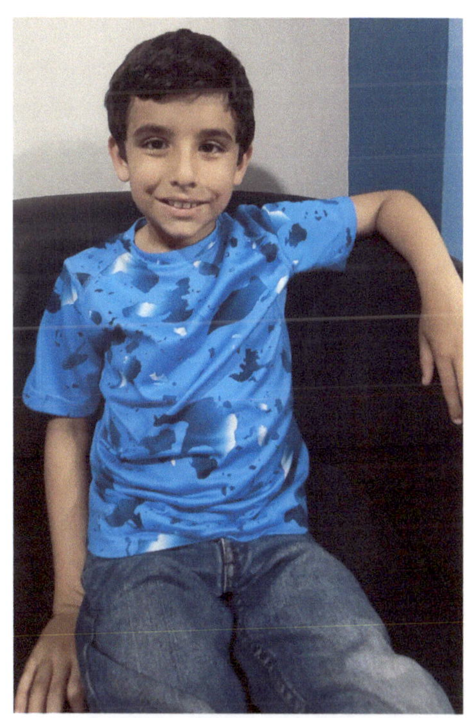

RAFAEL LORETO